Hindsight with Hollie:
The Poetic Journal

HOLLIE STONE

Copyright © 2022 Hollie Stone
All rights reserved
First Edition

Fulton Books, Inc.
Meadville, PA

Published by Fulton Books 2022

ISBN 979-8-88505-277-1 (paperback)
ISBN 979-8-88505-278-8 (digital)

Printed in the United States of America

Butterflies

Sometimes I get scared to try things that are new
To my people in heaven, it's all for you
I've got to stay positive even when skies aren't blue
That I'd be this far in life is something that I never knew

There are times when I get butterflies
God has given me some great highs
I think it's heaven's lights
Flying far up like kites

My mind and my heart sometimes disagree
My mind says don't be so nice, because then people will just use me
Yet my heart does opposite, as kindness is always key

All humans have some sort of *mystery* in their life story, with their own beautiful imperfections and flaws, of course. You see, there will come a time when you think everyone has heard about the mystery in your story, but there will always be someone who hasn't heard about it yet. So, never stop telling it. More often than not, we think that certain things we cannot control in our lives will rob us of the chance at a normal life. There is absolutely no such thing as a normal or perfect life, just like there is no such thing as a perfect human or a perfect story. We are all just a bunch of people trying to make the best of what time we have left in our lives. Mistakes are made by all, but what really matters is how and if we take it upon ourselves to learn from those mistakes.

Different Kind of Girl

She is an old soul
Has a unique rock to her roll
The smallest things make her heart feel whole

Knowing that life isn't perfect, she doesn't ask for perfection
One thing she'll always believe in is God's protection
She'll always be there to help when you lose direction

Anxiety can sometimes get the best of her
Just wanted to make sure you got home safe from where you were
In her mind, confrontation is one of the worst things to ever occur

Often giving the benefit of the doubt
Wanting to help everyone get through that rough spout
That's what life is all about

Different kind of girl
Whose heart can sometimes get thrown for a whirl
With an old soul and a unique twirl

As a female, it's so hard to remember to stop and love myself sometimes. I'll tell you one thing that hurts the people that you love is seeing you not love yourself. We often feel as if other people's judgment and criticism will be the death of us, when really it can be our own. The mirror is otherwise known as the self-judgment space. Where all the looks and thoughts happen, is where self-love is supposed to radiate. In all reality, not a single person in your circle will judge your looks, because they truly love you as a person. The best advice I could give someone in this day and time is to do what will make you happiest, and whoever stays with you through that journey are the ones you need to hang on to, not the ones who stay behind and wait for you to give up. It is indeed easy to hang on to old memories and let them draw you back to people, but life is way too short to be doing that anymore. There should never come a day that you feel guilty for doing what makes you the happiest in the end.

Push Through

Hey there
Nobody cares about what you wear
It doesn't even matter if you have greasy hair
What truly matters is your love and care

Your freckles make you stand out
That caring soul of yours is what life is all about
You should never be in self-doubt
It's okay to cry some things out

People will do you wrong
They'll string you along
But don't ever forget the words to your own song
Don't stay stuck on the little things too long

It's not all about a perfect pretty face
Or having a skinny waist
Who cares if someone doesn't like your taste
You have to push through and walk with pride in all you face

When I wrote this, I specifically wrote it for younger girls. I understand that once you start transitioning from a young child to a teenager it can seem difficult. It's that time in life when you start to realize that not everyone in the world is nice, but you can't let that stop you from growing and evolving. Use this time for self-discovery, find yourself, and have fun. Everyone isn't supposed to be just alike, because then the world would be boring. Be the real you, and don't ever change for anyone.

Better You

Life can definitely catch up to us
It can cause a big fuss
We can't help but board the struggle bus

We get busy putting others first
All of a sudden we'll unintentionally just burst
When nothing is going right it can make us feel cursed

A lot of us are full of so much hope
Never wanting to give up because we feel like we
are so close to grabbing that finish rope
Truthfully that can lead us down a slippery slope

Hope can sometimes outshine self-control
Don't ever let it dig too deep and put you in a hole
It should never change your beautiful soul

Once in a while you need to put those things aside
Let God do his amazing work and provide
Walk with gracious pride

It's okay to sit back and do what you want to do
Others don't even have to have a clue
As long as you remember to do what's better for you

Life can get so hectic and crazy sometimes, it's hard to remember to take care of yourself. No matter how busy it might get, please put yourself first once in a while. When you give yourself the short end of the stick, you can't do the things that you need to or take care of others because you end up drained. You deserve love too; you always will.

Small Circle

I have a small circle, and I like it that way
It's something I'll never be ashamed to say
I'm glad the friends I have are true friends that'll stay

When you have a larger group of friends respect is harder to build
It's never really sealed
Because there's a number you're trying to yield

It's harder to build respect because you're spreading
yourself thin between each person
Sadly that'll only make things worsen
That could leave you or other people hurting

You don't have to have a certain number of
friends to have friends that love you
You just have to find a few that do
True friends will be with you until you're old and gray too

    There is so much potential in a quantity as small as one person. Next time you stand in front of a mirror beating yourself up for being different, remember that. Remember that you are as delicate as a broken mirror, yet you carry everlasting beauty like a diamond. I get it. In a society like this one, we are faced with so much pure pressure. Feeling like we need to hop on a trend just because someone else did. People will definitely have similarities here and there, but we weren't created exactly the same, nor does that need to change. Popularity isn't worth anything. It's not real and true like a single friendship. It's not worth the stab in the back or the missing of opportunities. Honestly, if you can't comfortably act stupid around your friends, they aren't the friends for you. A true friend loves another for who they are without any add-ons or accessories. Friends accept flaws, and flaws create the best of friends. Keep the friend who tells you that you're crazy for saying such terrible things about yourself, not the friend that will endlessly agree with you. The best friendships are simple and free; don't forget that.

Let Things Happen

Some things come at your preferred time
Other things might come at the wrong time
Some of the best things come unexpectedly

You can make a wish and it might come true in that moment
Or you can make a wish, and it'll take a while to come true
God will make things happen when he feels they are meant to

Try not to stress over those things
They will happen if it's meant for you
Just let things happen

God answers all prayers; it just takes time. Sometimes, God waits a while to answer your prayer, because there's something he wants you to experience or see first. He never wants any of us to stress; we just have to pray and put the situation in his hands. Leaving it up to him is the best thing to do, because he always looks out for us better than anyone else.

Can't Believe It

I'm nowhere near perfect
Life is crazy, and I'm still trying to learn it
On the hard days I can't quit
Even if I'm down in the pit

I'll get frustrated with myself and wonder if I'm doing things right
I'll look around and see a glorious sight
My family is what reminds me to not be so stressed and uptight
They're my strength and light

At times I'm in denial
I'll sit and ponder
Why God chose me is something I often wonder
The blessings always outshine the thunder

I've had my fair share of failure
I'm still here because of my savior
I hit my knees in prayer
Thankful for another day here

Life is in no way perfect, easy, or ordinary. It is constantly changing, just like how the earth is constantly moving. Life won't ever stop, so we can't stop either. On those days when life feels impossible to handle, remember that you are worth so much more than you will ever know, and you should forever hold optimism and enthusiasm within that. Fight your battles with your own truths, light your fire with your own magic, and create your masterpiece using your own true colors. Even if we need a few reminders sometimes, we can never forget these things. Holding so much importance, these things are what hurt us most, what make us smile more, and what make us stronger.

Beautifully Bizarre

Having a good heart doesn't mean you're always strong
Some things will still go wrong
It's when we choose to pick ourselves up instead of dragging along

Having an open mind doesn't mean that you
don't get scared to try new things
It means you are always willing to handle whatever life brings
There are still things that might tug at your heartstrings

Being sensitive doesn't always mean you are weak
Holding in your emotions can sometimes cause them to leak
Some of us need occasional validation that others might not seek

A special soul
Kindness is the main goal
With emotions that ride along in the console

One trait doesn't define who you are
Behind a once broken heart there will always lie a scar
A good heart is beautifully bizarre

This poem is probably one of my favorite poems I have ever written. Every heart is different, just like every human. A good heart can be sensitive, closed off, wild, broken, carefree, and so much more. The similarity in every heart is that every heart is beautifully bizarre. Everyone has their own story and their own experiences that shape them into the person that they are and the heart that they have. If you're going to do anything in this life, use your heart to try and see the good and spread kindness wherever you go.

Strong for You

I knew in my heart in that very moment that I'd never be the same
You weren't to blame
Your time had came

Some days I feel a sense of relief knowing you're no longer in pain
Other days it drives me emotionally insane
It's a feeling I could never explain

I know it's something I'll never heal from
It's something you'd want me to try to overcome
Oh how I miss the sound of your sweet hum

Missing you will forever be an understatement of how I feel
Every day it feels a little more real
It's not an easy deal

I never realized just how much strength you gave me all along
I promise I'll try not to do anything wrong
Just like you always told me I'll be strong

    I have gone back and forth about sharing this one in my book, but here it is. I wrote this a little over a month after my grandmother's passing, and still to this day it's a thousand percent accurate. Grief is hard to deal with, hard to understand, and everything in between. If you are dealing with loss, my heart goes out to you. If someone you know is dealing with loss, please be patient and gentle. Grief is something that cannot be controlled. It truly never gets easier; the only thing we can do is use the memories we have to get us through each day. We must try to find the smallest amount of peace possible.

Easier Said than Done

Everyone dances to the beat of their own drum
Some have a heart as sweet as a plum
Others are a little numb

Never ask someone to change their beat
Try to put yourself in their seat
Just like you they are trying to make ends meet

People say be kind because it's what God intended
I don't think that phrase is ever fully comprehended
Kindness is the magic of life and on it's simple act we all depend

I know it's easier said than done
But don't tell that girl to take her messy hair out of that bun
Don't tell that guy that he needs to go for a run

    We can't control what others do, but we can think about things before we say them, hug a little tighter, and face our fears. Once you say something hurtful to someone, it could possibly stick with them forever and create a fear within them like no other, and no one deserves to be treated like that. There is only one person who will ever walk on water, so we shouldn't think for one second that we do. With that being said, don't ever let people treat you any way they want to and have you thinking they run your show. You will always own the right to stand up for yourself, and you will always own the right to do what's best for you.

Find Me

In life we'll have to make decisions that are tough
They'll sometimes leave our hearts feeling rough
Though we knew that had gone on long enough

It'll hurt for a little while
You'll feel like your heart has run a mile
But don't ever lose your reason to smile

There will be emotional breakdowns
Inner guilt takedowns
A few nervous shakedowns

You'll ask yourself if it was the right thing to do
Just remember that it was a decision you made for you
When it's all over you'll feel brand new

This has happened to me
I was farther up in the clouds than the eye could see
It took time but I just had to go find me

    I understand how you feel; I was once there too. Sometimes we just get in a funk and lose ourselves, it's human nature and it's something we can't help. Life gets in the way, but you can't stop living, growing, and learning. I firmly believe that growth is one of the most beautiful things there is. There's no greater feeling than learning who you are and what you love most about life. Being a selfless person is such a wonderful kind of person to be, but you must still continue to do what is best for you. No matter what you go through in life, remember that you are worth so much. You deserve to be yourself, know yourself, and most importantly, you deserve to love yourself.

Unpredictable

I have my good and bad days
Sometimes my voice takes an unnecessary raise
I like to look at hard times as if they are just a phase

I sometimes get nervous to try new things
I'm also open to see what life brings
I like the way a spring hummingbird sings

I can have a lot to say or say nothing at all
My life doesn't always look like that perfect picture on the wall
A six-o'clock sunset is one of the prettiest things I've ever saw

I make a lot of mistakes
But in life there are no retakes
A smile could be on my face the moment my heart breaks

Being a disappointment is one of my worst fears
I hope the reality of that never nears
I have people in heaven who need me to be fierce

I enjoy the little things in life
I believe we shouldn't hold onto strife
I feel that kindness is like a light and hate is like a knife

Sometimes complicated
Yet simple
Oh so unpredictable

It Isn't Assured

Time always goes by fast
That's why it's best to put the little unnecessary fights in the past
Make memories that'll last

You can't help but be scared for tomorrow
Pay attention to what parts of yourself that you let people borrow
I know that sometimes you can't help but drown in sorrow

Don't let something so small turn into something large
Remember that we can't always be right or in charge
Sadly there are some batteries you can never recharge

There is so much power in a gesture as small as a hug
Use words when talking instead of a shrug
Just because you might be upset with someone doesn't
mean you should sweep them under the rug

Tomorrow is never assured sadly
So try not to treat people too badly
Always leave a situation gladly

One day, you'll miss the opportunity to go see your grandparents, cousins, and other family members. You'll find yourself wishing you would've hugged someone just a little tighter. Speaking from experience, I have found myself wishing I would have thought about something a little more in-depth before I said it. Emotions can get the best of us in a hard situation, but the best thing we can do is try to find something positive within that and try to leave it gladly with good intentions. My point is no matter how boring you might think it is, please spend time with your loved ones while you still have them, try to think a little more about the things you say before you speak, and try to find the good in every situation.

It'll Be All Right

If you're pregnant and nervous to bring your
little one into this crazy world we live in
Hold your head high because there is courage within
I can only imagine what a stressful nine months it's been
It'll all be worth it when you see that grin

If you're a mom to a teenager
I know we can act immature
That's just our nature
We are learning to independently adventure

If you're a worried or struggling parent
That doesn't at all make you boring or generic
It's understandable that you are hysteric
You aren't pathetic

If you are going through a tough situation
I know it feels like a steady beating vibration
For you I have absolute admiration
One day you'll be able to break free without hesitation

Whatever you might be going through just try to
keep your head up and try to see the light
I understand that you're putting up one heck of a fight
It's hard to hang tight
You will conquer this, and everything will be all right

It Won't Be Perfect

Some things only God knows
You'll experience some of the highest highs and lowest lows
There's going to be days that you just want to fall to your toes

In an uncertain time
Together you must climb
A relationship can't be fixed with tequila and lime

Always remember to listen to one another
Hold each other
Never let others hover

You can only protect so many of your emotions
There will be some commotion
It isn't just a title but a devotion

You are never finished learning
Be strong and don't allow those bridges to start burning
Stay true to what the two of you have created
and keep the wheel turning

Before making decisions you must reflect
Show each other a little respect
Be each other's strength because it'll never be exactly perfect

There isn't and will never be a single perfect relationship. It's not supposed to be perfect; you just have to choose who the best person is for you to struggle and make memories with. The right one won't expect you to be anyone other than yourself. Love is built on faith, respect, and loyalty.

One Thing I Ask

There's only one thing I could ever ask for
That the Lord hold me when I want to hit the floor
That he'll open up a new door

When my heart is broken
He'll throw me a strengthening token
I pray that I'll forever remain outspoken

Give me the strength to swim through deep waters
To always keep a smile on my face
Help me to remember to always give others a little bit of grace

Protect the ones for which I have love and care
Fill their days with laughter and don't leave them bare
Please walk them through life as delicately as
possible and don't try to pull hair

I have called on God so many times, whether it's for the good of myself or others. You see, I'm a quiet prayer. I choose to pray after everyone has left the room, I choose to pray by myself. I feel like some of my deepest connections with God have been made when I'm by myself. I don't read the Bible near as much as I should, but I know he is the reason why I have always gotten that one thing I ask for his protection. As I have previously mentioned, God answers every prayer when he feels it is the right time for that prayer to be answered. Leaving your worries in his hands is the best thing you could ever do.

What I Live For

One of my biggest goals is to make people smile
You never know if it's been a while
It's as simple as complimenting their style

To others I want to be a source of kindness and help
You never know with what someone has dealt
I try to make sure that when I leave there was love felt

I live to see others' happiness
It leaves me overjoyed and speechless
It makes me feel as if I've fulfilled my purpose
not perfectly but I at least tried my best

One of the greatest things someone can do is to simply be kind. Kindness and the little things come hand in hand. You'd be surprised at what a small act of kindness can do; it could move mountains for someone and make quite the impact on their life. Never stop being you, and never stop being kind. This crazy world we live in could definitely use some more kindness in it.

Some Things

We're all human
We sometimes take on tasks like we're superman
There are some things we think we know like the back of our hand

But there's some things that life brings
Might tear our heart into strings
Makes us do a full circle around rings

We sometimes say stuff that can sound a little rough
We can only be so tough
Somebody might even call your bluff

There are some things that even honesty and kindness cannot fix
Inner and outer conflicts
Unnecessarily beating ourselves up like a ton of bricks

We all make mistakes; we are all human. There are some things that we just can't control no matter how hard we try, and that isn't our fault. Rest easy at night knowing you are giving it your all and trying your best. Don't be too hard on yourself either, because everything will be alright in the end.

Wild Heart

I have a wild heart
It isn't an art
I guess you could say it's just something I carry along in my cart

I'm a little fun and crazy
A little hazy
A little sweet like old Ms. Daisy

I joke around from time to time
Out of every battle I must climb
Never afraid of a little dirt and grime

I wear my heart on my sleeve
In kindness I believe
What you give you shall receive

The Girl I Am

I drive recklessly
Always looking a little messy
Trying to always act selflessly

I'd rather wear sweats
Always have my hair in a bun that's quite a mess
Sometimes I stress

Some might think I'm a little brutal
I think honesty is deserved by all
Always there to help when you call

I don't care to drip in finesse
I don't have anyone to impress
Just a simple hot mess express

    This is one of the very first poems I had ever wrote, but it still says a lot about me. I'm not perfect, and I'll never expect perfection. Don't you ever worry about what people might say or think about you, because all that will ever truly matter is if you are happy and doing what is best for you.

Little Girl

To all the little girls
Your heart will be thrown for a few whirls
There might even be some baton twirls

Enjoy those moments freely running through the grass
Show every bit of sass your little heart has
Get creative with things, and add your own pizzazz

Run across that bitty ball court like a Curry
You're going to miss those days where you have not even one worry
Don't be in such a hurry

Be kind, but don't let others put you in a hole
Love with all of your heart and soul
Strive to reach your goal

Guard your ever so precious heart
Create your own magical art
Never be too hard on yourself sweetheart

While you're young and little enjoy the carbs and rice
Stay wild little one
Just a little advice

I wrote this on July 16, 2020 and dedicated it to my grandmother. When I was a little girl, we would chase each other through the grass, throw the football around, and have our own little picnics. I'd do anything to go back to those days; all I could think about at that age was growing up. Don't wish those years away, because once you start to grow up life becomes a whole lot more complicated.

Maybe It's What He Wanted

I have a hard time trusting folks
Nowadays life is full of fake people and their jokes
It's almost as if they think others' feelings are a hoax

I also have hope and believe in the power of change
But there are some people who will never rearrange
We don't think of how certain things might
affect others this day and age

I often think I'm doing something in life wrong
I wonder if it's just that God didn't want
certain people in my life too long
My faith in his plan will forever remain strong

I continue to try and see the good in God's creation
But for people to change is a dream that I'll no longer be chasing
Now and always kindness has a spot in my heart
that nothing will ever come close to replacing

Sometimes God removes people from your life for the better, even if you don't notice that right away. Pray about it, be kind about it, and move on. You might never find out exactly why, but just trust in his plan, and it will definitely all make sense someday.

"Kindness Moves Mountains"

No, I am not the first person to say that. I stumbled across that beautiful quote a few years ago, and I have tried to live by it, and repeat it to others ever since. How can kindness move mountains, you might ask? That's a great question.

A lot of people choose to fight their battles in silence, which most likely equals silent suffering. An act of kindness as small as opening a door or telling someone to have a good day could give that person one more reason to keep holding on. Reminding someone of all the amazing reasons they need to stay here can be the reason that they decide not to leave. Encouraging someone to keep pushing forward in their success could be the reason they continue to chase their biggest dream of all. Little things can do big things, too.

When you think of doing something kind, your first thought is probably paying for someone's meal or their drink. That's great, but even an action smaller than that can do something for someone. You might think that giving someone a gift is a huge act of kindness, and it is in a way. Rather than giving someone a materialistic gift, give them the gift of kindness by action or words. I am the giving type, but I am also the type of person who is always there with the gift of advice, a listening ear, and a shoulder to cry on when it's asked for.

The two awesome things about kindness are that it's free and it can be shown in many different ways. This way, anyone and everyone have the ability to show kindness wherever they might go. When I tell you that quote changed my life, it made me see and think about things from a completely different perspective. I started to think about every time someone has opened a door for me, given me a compliment, offered me some advice, and so much more. Be the reason that mountains are moved, and spread kindness wherever you go.

Happiness is a Mood; Positivity is a Mindset.

This is another one of my all-time favorite quotes. My seventh-grade English teacher shared this with my fellow classmates and me one day; it spoke volumes to me. At first, it took me a few reads to completely understand it.

Isn't happiness a mindset too, you might ask? That's a wonderful question; let's discuss it. In order to find and achieve your own happiness, you have to try your absolute hardest to find the good in every situation. You have to keep a positive outlook on life. I know, I'm guilty of doing the exact opposite too. Something that I've had to learn is that you can't depend on anyone else but yourself to make you happy; otherwise it won't last.

To answer the question. Happiness is the mood that you'll stay in when you keep a positive mindset. Keeping a positive mindset will allow happiness to come your way. Stay positive, set boundaries, and give yourself some grace. Keeping a positive outlook can do so much good for your soul and your happiness too.

About the Author

Hollie Stone is a small-town poet, blogger, and full-time high school student. She started writing poetry in early 2019, and she has since had so many people tell her that she should write a book of some sort. In this book, you will read some of her most popular and inspiring poetry. Every poem she has written is based on her true and personal experiences in life. She just put those things on paper and hopes that it'll inspire someone. This is the first book of her series; the next one will be a little different. She hopes that whoever reads this book enjoys it, can relate to it, and find peace in it as well.

You have a purpose, you are loved, you are strong, and you can absolutely do anything that you set your mind to. Do what makes you happy. Hug your loved ones tightly, and make as many beautiful memories as you can. Most importantly, dream big and never give up.

CPSIA information can be obtained
at www.ICGtesting.com
Printed in the USA
JSHW021724090622
26816JS00002B/109